AMERICA 2000

FOUNDATIONS FOR GENERATIONS!
The Making Of The American Party Of America/AOA

"The Party That Empowers You-The Working Family In America"

Second Printing

ISBN 10:0615844537
ISBN 13:978-0615844534

DEDICATIO

*"THIS BOOK IS DEDICATED TO ANDREW & ELEANOR BALL
FOR WHOM I RECEIVED MY TRAINING FOR LIFE"*

ACKNOWLEDGMENTS:

"I WANT TO PERSONALLY THANK ALL THOSE
WHO PARTICIPATED IN THE MAKING OF
THIS BOOK PROJECT & ASSISTED
TO PRODUCE, PRINT,
MARKET & DISTRIBUTE.
SPECIAL THANKS
GOES TO:
CIERRA HUDNALL
DESIGN
SUPPORT!"

<>

AMERICA 2000: Foundations For Generations!
TABLE OF CONTENTS & SUMMARY OF TOPICS:

PART II - <u>ECONOMIC STRANGULATION UPON AMERICAN WORKER & TRADITIONAL MIDDLE CLASS FAMILY!</u>

PART III - <u>REDEFINING AMERICA!</u>
<u>"THE NATION MUST PROTECT ITSELF!"</u>

by: Dennis Andrew Ball, Founder/AOA, Chairman/ANC

& 2016 Candidate For President Of the United States!

Essay 1. PROLOGUE: Introduction -18 Essays

Including *President Kennedy's Final Speech,

Dallas, Texas - November 22, 1963!

"Shall We Gather Together With One Voice

With One Purpose With One Direction, To

Bring Our People Together And Make Our

Democracy Work To Preserve, Protect And

Defend The Most Basic Of Social Institutions:

THE TRADITIONAL AMERICAN WORKING FAMILY

& THE AMERICAN FREE ENTERPRISE SYSTEM

THAT MAKES IT WORK!"

This is the revised Edition of America 2000:

Foundations For Generations! The first edition

was written in 1995 just in time for the 1996

Presidential Election between United States

Senator Robert Dole (R-KS) and President Wm.

Jefferson Clinton, Bill Clinton, 42nd President

of the United State of America. Now, as then,

OUR Nation is facing other crisis and challenges

created by those with others who disregard

basic to our rights and values regarding Children,

Parents and Grandparents, the traditional family;
it is because of the "growing up" into maturity
that this 3rd Party initiative has Come of Age.

Throughout our nations' history, crisis has
always seemed to define its destiny. Now as
then, the American Family is under assault in
many ways, both economically and culturally
like no time in History the seismic shifts in
opinion and actions detrimental to its health,
preservation, protection and good will for the
traditional family; values of truth, honor,
sustainability and transparency between
members and those who would find fault and
and deviate from that standard rooted in Social
Injustice & Officials elected by the populace
to serve them rather than in control over them.

a). My concerns are rooted in what I perceive
as a growing alienation of American Values
that puts people second & social institutions 1st!
This cannot be in a civilized society rooted
in Republican Democracy. Republican meaning the
Republic of the United States of America One Nation
Under God Indivisible With Liberty & Justice For All!

b). If an Socialist elite is allowed to take control, they will
strangle to death the American family both economically
and personally creating hostility within the Corporate
Culture trickling down into the inner workings of family
members causing unnecessary conflicts and loss of

respect amongst their members. If ever there was a
time to Call Out This Menace To American Democracy,

IT IS NOW!"

c). History has proven that how goes the family
in America goes the Country as a whole. This story
is rooted in what has put us here and "Where as
a Society are we going?" Question that!
Problem is that there is now a void and leadership
vacuum in the nation that calls for **We The People**
To Fill! At this inaugural opportunity, our hope is to
start the process of dialogue about Accountability
& Transparency, Reform & Justice amongst those
inside the Country & State Governments including
those who profit by criminal means to exploit, plunder,
pilfer and pillage the Vulnerable and Displaced families
and those who are placed within Court Supervision
by appointed Guardians, Conservators and Nursing
Staff who violate their Constitutional Due Process
Rights With Impunity making folly our lives, honor;
and fortunes. This is totally **UNACCEPTABLE!**

d). I wish to introduce and reflect on the problems
& solutions that have created anarchy in the midst
of a Country founded on the principle of
"Domestic Tranquility" yet it seems as though WE
the American People are exploited everyday by
BIG Government and a Corrupt State & Federal
Bureaucracy that fails to honor the Bill of Rights
and the Constitiutional Guarantees established
by the founders of our great Constitutional Republic!

8   e). In the following essays, you will see the
     condition of our culture, how we got here and what
     must be done to reign in years of cultural abuse
     eminating from all sides of the American Experiment
     in a post WWII era and economy showing how far
     we have moved away from our cultural & constitutional
     principles of life, liberty & the pursuit of happiness by
     the very institutions that were established to make life
     in America the most attractive of all societies in the
     World! President Kennedy in his unspoken speech the
     day he died in Dallas, Texas spoke of America's heritage
     & destiny as a City on a Hill to guide the world in a Post
     World War II America back to prosperity and leadership
     for the World to marvel at its production capacity to not
     only support its people but to advance initiatives for the
     betterment of all mankind throughout the World and its
     families. That Speech is reproduced for your review in
     Essay Seventeen.

     "The Free Enterprise Capitalistic Economic System
     With Its Millions Of Decision Makers Is The Foundational
     Democratic Institution In America" - Sen. Jim Demint (R-SC)
     (from his book: "Saving Freedom")

PART 1-THE DEBT CRISIS! EMERGENCY! EMERGENCY!

Essay 2: JOBS! JOBS! JOBS! Protecting the American Worker!

Corporatism Equals Socialism vs. Free Enterprise Capitalism!

" Why Can't We All Just Get Along?" - Rodney King, (1992)

The founder of Capitalism, Adam Smith believed that essential to monetary policy to support society required that capital from banking was necessary inorder to create the ends or results for the American Working or Middle Class. Since the introduction of America into the World Economy and during the G8 Economic Summits beginning in the early 70's with the Nixon trip to China, the means have not justified the ends at all. As a matter of fact, the ends have been so lopsided that the United States Imports more than it Exports. Now, why is this I ask you? Let's get real people! Everyone of us should be OUTRAGED!; inspite that the United States out produced the World to Win World War II on two continents, our nation finds itself in the cross-hairs of Corporate Global Expansionism created by Corporations not loyal to the American Working Middle Class! Their loyalties divided by their Wall Street share holders and stock investors. The same people who have caused the Mortgage Bust & Sky Rocketing Unemployment to Persist! These are the same kind of people whom in 1832, President Andrew Jackson fought at the Bank of the U.S., European Bankers tied to American Capital using the dollar to prop up the Euro as China props up the Federal Reserve with a doomsday scenario sounding like dominos falling on the Dow.

It is only a matter of time until or unless the very economic underpinnings of sound monetary and fiscal policy gives way and the entire economic system comes crashing down on the entire World!

The facts are these, unless or until the manufacturing slogan, "MADE IN AMERICA" is once again re-established for Middle AMERICANS, the notion that multiculturalism can work in a pluralistic society becomes only a fable and at best just a myth. The means of production must justify the ends and without capital coming to the people, there can and will be no ends of production, only pain and poverty created by an ugly selfish & arrogant elite of Social High Steppers within State & Federal Government owned by a minority Corporate Elite.

The Current Debt Crisis in the United States & Europe is a problem of EXTRAVAGANCE GONE WILD~! Like a PIG running free devouring everything it smells so Out-Of-Control spending jaunts by both State & Federal Officials have caused the American Worker pain at the Pump with excessive gasoline taxes to prop up local and state government. Food taxes to pay for declining revenues and the necessity for government to pay food stamps to its working poor some of which are sinking middle class families only compounds the problems of a nation OUT-OF-CONTROL!

I ask you, "How Long Can A Nation's Economy Be sustained by Over Indulgance & Declining Revenues?" How Long Can a Nation be propped up by the printing of paper money, some call it play money because its worth is based on the worth of its Government? Without the means to produce the ends of production, how long can a society care for itself without falling down on the Streets?

The World War II economy imposed rationing on itself in order to stretch commodities and food nutrients. Minerals

were allocated for WAR for a War Time Economy. The Nation
was United and Determined to WIN! Where are those who
say America Can Win Again!?

>"THINK 1ST WHAT OUR COUNTRY HAS BECOME:
>ACT & DO WHAT MUST BE DONE!"

IN SO DOING THE ATTITUDE OF PRODUCTION BECOMES
ONCE AGAIN THE DRIVING FORCE IN THE SOCIETY!
IT CAN A BE SAID THAT FREE ENTERPRISE CAPITALISM IS
THE ECONOMIC ENGINE OF THE MIDDLE CLASS AND MUST
NOT BE ALLOWED TO BE DAMAGED AT ANYTIME IN OUR
HISTORY BY CORPORATIONS WHO USE, ABUSE & MISUSE
THE MEANS OF PRODUCTION TO DAMAGE, INJURE AND
DESTROY THE HETEROSEXUAL NUCLEAR FAMILY!

"THE MEANS OF PRODUCTION MUST BE IN PLACE FOR
THE TRADITIONAL AMERICAN FAMILY TO SUCCEED!"

IT Can also be said, that the richest resource of any
nation are its own children. Yet, in too many instances,
our own children are treated like mere slaves without
consideration for their economic future or the financial
burden they MAY BARE? How Can a nation be sustained
on reckless abandon? THIS WILL REQUIRE TOUGH LOVE!

Essay 3. Business, Labor & Government: A Change In
Thinking To Assist The Breakdown of the Working Family
And The Punishment For Doing A Good Job!

Shakespeare made several references to the tragedies in life that are unavoidable. In family life, the same is true only multiplied by those having to bare the brunt of it. Of course, inspite of being a good worker, it goes without saying that only a good employer can take satisfaction in having a labor force rewarded and motivated.

At one time in America, that attitude rang supreme as the wheels of a production economy demanded war time speed to meet the deadlines of munitions and armaments in all services. That was the model for the American Economy until Corporations & their Shareholders GOT IN THE WAY! Add multilateralism and you have the recipe for disaster that 25 million unemployed in America are living off government food stamps and emergency room care while the nations of the world are out producing and out sourcing jobs from America to themselves by Corporate Insiders headquartered in foreign countries but doing business in America to avoid high corporate taxes which turns out they don't pay anyway.

The treasonous conduct of American Business has become a problem in a Global Economy.

"MADE IN AMERICA" has become a myth of our past for a number of reasons.

Foreign currencies and investment back in America must become the norm once again protecting a free market by free enterprise principles and tools must be employed by business, labor and government for the welbeing and good will of the traditional heterosexual nuclear family!

Essay 4: MADE IN AMERICA! - MADE IN AMERICA!
A Production Economy Vs. An Economy of Consumerism!

Why is the United States having so much trouble sustaining its Economy? Could it be that the United States is MAXED its CREDIT and WE THE PEOPLE with it? Could it be that the age of limitless CONSUMERISM has caught up with American Cultural Society? That the means of production has not kept up with the ends of production? Could it be that the turbulent struggles the American Middle Class are faced is a result of uncaring Corporations and Politicians who see themselves as Social & Economic Elitists at the Controls of Production & Spending? That a job well done is actually punished by Bosses Who Have Little or NO Regard for their employees and those they Supervise? To destroy the Self-esteem in the American Family is NO BIG Deal because labor is easily replaceable?

These are IMPORTANT QUESTIONS that MUST Be Asked! To not do so would be as equally Sinister as those who commit Social Evil and at a torrrid pace everyday! Children suffer for lack of support by parents who are cancelled by Corporations who have an uncaring, negative attitude toward the American Family. For this Country to survive it must also have a caring people within its institutions and corporations. How goes the family So goes the United States!

"Think 1st What Our Country Has Become,

Act & Do What Must Be Done!"

And Now I Ask, What Must Be Done To Change A Consumer Society To That Of One Centered Around The Means of Production?

Could it be that Americans MUST DEMAND MORE FROM THEIR OFFICIALS IN SUPPORT OF THEMSELVES & THEIR FAMILY'S ECONOMY? IS IT POSSIBLE THAT THE WORKING CLASS WILL MORPH INTO A SUB-CLASS WITH NO PARENTAL SUPERVISION OR INCENTIVE TO DO BETTER FOR OURSELVES & ALLOW THE STATE TOTAL CONTROL OVER OUR DAILY LIVES?

IS THAT THE COUNTRY YOU WANT TO SEE IN THE FUTURE? FOR YOU & YOUR CHILDREN? DO YOU WANT TO SEE THE ORGANS OF POWER SLIP AWAY INTO OBLIVION BY THE VIOLENT OVERTHROW OF ITS INSTITUTIONAL SYSTEMS LIKE THOSE IN THE MIDDLE EAST AND EUROPE? THIS WILL REQUIRE THAT WE GET BUSY AND DO WHAT IS NECESSARY TO AVERT A TOTAL & COMPLETE ECONOMIC AND SOCIAL DISASTER PLACING THE UNITED STATES UNDER MARSHALL LAW BY PRESIDENTIAL ORDER. WE ARE FAST APPROACHING A POINT IN TIME WHERE THE MEANS OF PRODUCTION MUST BEGIN TO RE-EMERGE ITSELF FOR FAMILY SAKE WITHIN THE UNITED STATES!

MADE IN AMERICA MUST ONCE AGAIN BECOME THE NORM; NOT THE EXCEPTION! AMERICAN EXCEPTIONALISM IN A GLOBAL ECONOMY MUST ONCE AGAIN COME FORTH!

Is it fair that American products are taxed by foreign countries importing into their country products made in the United States? NO, IT'S NOT! The trading relationships the United States has with China is an imbalanced one created by American and Multinational Corporations who trade with no import restrictions on China. As a consequence, America's economic means of production has been damaged because of these imbalanced corporate and national relationships with Beijing, China.

The parents who raise the children and require the means of production to support them, find themselves competing in a losing battle of competitive struggle for a job they can depend on to support their children and themselves. Corporations have used China & Other Countries to make money at the Expense of the traditional American Family and have done it with IMPUNITY!

This is a VIOLATION of Cannon Law of Economic Production! You don't destroy that which is an asset of Production in a Plural Society of Social Needs. Dissassembling American Factories by moving them to China has been a huge mistake for the parents of children in America! The means of production depend on not only a qualified work force but also an economy that is protected by its Officials, both Corporate & Government! For that alone, America must act to put MADE IN AMERICA back in the mainstream of Production.

"Think 1st What Our Country Has Become,

Act & Do What Must Be Done!"

Essay 5: Globalization - A Failed Policy: Low Job Skills
Won't Work Turning Out Psychotics, Alcoholics, Drug
Addicts & Workaholics! "Free Trade" A Complete &
Total Disaster For The Traditional American Working
Family!

So far, troubling as it may seem, we haven't even
scratched the surface of that which must be corrected
for our nation to survive let alone become a great nation
once again in order to thrive! The United States for years
enjoyed a position of strength from having and holding the
"means of production" as the world's leader of import and
export products - especially during and after the Second
World War.

But with the advent of the Cold War and a changing
Global Identity between the nations of Business, Labor
& Government, all of that changed with the advent of
Globalization as a FAILED POLICY within the context of
the traditional American Family Unit.

What once was common and taken for granted as a
way of life continued to place undue stress on WORKING
FAMILIES who's means of support was to Work & Save,
Work & Save, Work & Save!

Problem was and is that no matter how long or hard

you Work & Save, this government always has found a
way to keep the working family poor or on a fine line of
insolvency or near insolvency to fund all of their Budgets
and Wasteful Spending; which consequently created a
pattern of slave indenturedhood impacting the quality of
life once envied by the World about the American Worker
and family! Economist Hernando DeSoto of Peru knows.

Now, mental health becomes a Working Class problem.
Mental Health has become a top priority today in dealing with
Global Economic Crisis impacting the United States. Death
is common place from the onslaught of uncaring Corporations
who use America as a platform without consideration of its
labor force including State & Federal Governments whom have
removed themselves from the one-on-one crisis of everyday
people struggling with debt they cannot cope outside of taking
Bankruptcy!

As a consequence, the financial insecurity this produces for
them and those in their family is overwhelming creating:
Psychotics, Neurotics, Alcoholics, Drug Addicts and Workaholics!
This is UNACCEPTABLE! A Great Nation Will Not ALLOW
ITS OWN PEOPLE TO SUFFER At The Hands of other's Morbid
Depravity!

"AMERICA MUST DO BETTER! "WE CAN! WE WILL!"

Unfortunately, DOING A GOOD JOB IN AMERICA TODAY,
MAY get you fired because you did. What kind of people
have we become?

I want to answer the questions asked here to consider

what has been proposed by emerging the "means of production" as the working person's solution. It goes without saying that "low skills" won't work either inorder to support oneself and their family. The days of indentured servitude have arrived back to the United States because its Institutions and People have let and allowed it!

THIS MUST CHANGE! & THIS MUST STOP!
"BUT HOW YOU ASK DO YOU?"

Certainly by not hiring more government jobs on limited State & Federal Budgets that are starved due to administrative and budgetary constraints. No, it will take much more than this to find our nation out of this HOLE that was created for WE THE PEOPLE! IT WILL REQUIRE ENLISTING THE FINEST MINDS OF AMERICAN INGENUITY TO GROW REVENUES BACK INTO FULL EMPLOYMENT WITH THE MEANS OF PRODUCTION!

"IT WILL REQUIRE CORPORATIONS, BANKS, SMALL BUSINESSES, TRADE TARIFFS, TO INVEST BACK IN AMERICA FROM WHAT THEY HAVE BENEFITTED FROM AND BY AMERICA!" & "THAT GOVERNMENT OF THE PEOPLE, BY THE PEOPLE & FOR THE PEOPLE" WILL BE AFFIRMED ONCE AGAIN IN ALL COUNTY, STATE & FEDERAL ACTS! AND DECISIONS!" The American Worker and traditional family is worth protecting! WE Americans have lost too much time and too much ground because of abuses by other people! Now, we must "take positive action" to correct the problems! AND CORRECT THEM NOW! WE MUST DEMAND

ACCOUNTABILITY & TRANSPARENCY BY ALL ELECTED OR APPOINTED OFFICIALS TO THE AMERICAN PEOPLE!

"THE HONOR THAT WAS LOST MUST BE FOUND!"

Essay 6: "Made In America": Made Myth By An Abusive Corporate Culture! RESULTING IN ECONOMIC STRANGULATION UPON WORKING FAMILY!

As was discussed in JOBS! JOBS! JOBS! ESSAY 2, American Corporations have played hugh administrative manuevers around the American Working Family in order to protect and preserve their shareholders at the expense of the American People and families. The Myth made in America in today's economy is correctly penned because of the hugh transfer of the "means of production" to other countries, primarily China but also with the participation of all the free trade nations that aspired to belong to NAFTA, the North American Free Trade Agreement signed under the close watch of the Clinton Administration.

FREE TRADE HAS BANKRUPT THE AMERICAN FAMILY FOR SEVERAL REASONS WHILE FAMILY MEMBERS STRUGGLE WITH ACCRUED & ACQUIRED DEBT WITH NO JOB! OUTRAGEOUS!

The Reasons for this are SEVERAL. They are:

1. INFLATION! The cost of living nearly yearly risen since the Clinton Administration took office in 1993.

2. ENERGY! Rather than change to a Fossil-Free economy, Lobbyists & Oil executives have paid to keep progress on energy independence from happening. The buildings that occupy Federal employees to manage the production of oil consumption & independence have failed the American People by allowing the cost of energy to satisfy those who control it. Once again, "the means of production!" This must STOP! America put a "LUNAR ROVER" on the moon with the Apollo Missions. Why can't that same technology be used on Earth? Solar Charging made simple with just one solar panel attached to a stationary binary object with power cord to the Vehicle is simple cheap & non-polluting! America produces about 7 million barrels of oil a day. We could actually have a surplus of oil if our nation put a renewable energy program IN MOTION NOW! More on this in Essay 11.

3. TRADE IMBALANCE BETWEEN IMPORT & EXPORT OF AMERICAN PRODUCTS TO NATIONS NOT FRIENDLY TO THE U.S. The dollar loses its value against countries who sell us their products & services at a rate we cannot compete in terms of production goals, costs and quotas. These Countries can cost us more for their imported non-tariffed goods while we must pay tariffs to export ours to them. This imbalance impacts the "cost of goods & services"

and produces more burdens for the American Family
to carry let alone the impact it has on our Gross
Domestic Product (GDP).

4. THE LINK BETWEEN TAX & SPEND & JOBS! More
   Government Programs, More Spending, More taxes,
   County, State & Federal Income taxes, Gas taxes,
   Sales taxes, Capital Gains taxes etc. The rate of
   taxation causes families to suffer because the cycle
   impacts business and labor. People want to work
   but they are taxed at a rate that they must work
   almost a half year strictly dedicated to paying their
   tax bills! THIS IS UNACCEPTABLE! OUT OF CONTROL
   GOVERNMENT SPENDING IS THE PROBLEM WITH
   BUREAUCRATS WHO FOLLOW ALONG TO GET ALONG!

(a). Following the personal tax rates is the cost for
     Corporate Income Tax Rates. Currently at 35%,
     however, many corporations pay **NO TAXES**
     because again of a distorted view that they can
     play musical chairs with the IRS in order to save
     their Company from paying their fair share. Adam
     Smith & John Adams believed that the "means of
     production" owed something for the "ends of
     production." Corporate income taxes are part of
     being an equitable partner in the Society where
     gains are made by the structures put in place.
     It also means paying their fair-share to lower the
     tax burden put on the families of America!

(b). However, in a bad economy, it is wise that they

pay a low rate flat tax on business net sales,

and on personal adjusted gross income.

With tariffs, Business now becomes an equitable

partner in creating jobs for working middle class

workers and families! ITS TIME TO RETURN TO

ECONOMICS! WITH ALL OF THESE UNACCOUNTED

ABUSES, IT IS NO WONDER "MADE IN AMERICA"

IS THE EXCEPTION RATHER THAN THE RULE.

THIS MUST CHANGE!

Essay 7: BUSINESS HIRES PEOPLE: Banks Provide Capital-

Government Regulates Banks & The Federal Reserve

Operates With Impunity! New Generals Required!

Throughout the discussion of the Debt Crisis, I have

attempted to point out the causes and effects of bad monetary

policy by the Organs of Power that have violated the "means

of production" in the United States. Now, we must direct our

attention to the independent agency that has tremendously

contributed to our crisis and economic problems. Our nation

has been previously warned that to allow foreign interests to

control American Monetary policy could be disasterous. The

debt crisis has caused these concerns to become a self fulfilling

policy until it is dealt with appropriately by both the President

& the Congress.

WHAT MUST BE DONE?

Early in the Nation's History, the Founders made it clear that Monetary interests outside of the United States could put at risk the young nation's growth and development and similarly find itself in the same position it was at the time of the American Revolution by becoming subservient to the Monetary Investments designed to control the "means of production" that Business, Labor & Government require to form and function for the American People. Those investments were made by foreign Bankers who's goals were to make loans and interest from them. However, the relationship of the Bank of the United States with wealthy industrialists caused tremendous divisions and conflicts within the ruling elite of America, so much so that President Andrew Jackson in 1829 formed the Democratic Party to fight and protect the monetary policy and financial interests of the Common Man and Women, including that of Children.

In essence what Jackson did was to tell the Bank of the United States to disband and go away. He paid off the debt with the Federal Treasury and closed down the Bank entirely! In effect, Jackson became a hero because he wouldn't allow foreign interests to hurt the American Economy by controlling monetary policy of the American People. America was spared the same fate other Countries encountered by allowing unsustainable debt to destroy their currency and financial system. However, America has not learned from its history and is now put in a vulnerable position by diluting its economic base for the working families of America!

Because Banks control the flow of capital the Federal

Reserve is their taskmaster!

Telling them what they will do with the funds they receive upon the Fed's Monetary Policy. But the Fed hasn't required they lend their funds to Small Business nor since the Bailouts to support Labor in getting people to work! Is that their job? ABSOLUTELY! WHY?

Because Banks have a duty in their Community to assist their Community in making a profit for their depositors who save with the Bank. The money they lend for honest services through Business, Labor & Government for the American Worker and Family! Banks have a duty to make loans that improve the quality of their Community & the Families who live in them! This must change. America is on economic tilt because of the hits she took by the mortgage bubble and the banking business being enamored in billions of dollars of bad debt! The CORRECTION of this debt is necessary to get money flowing again by monetary policies that encourage and create job creation by lower corporate taxes and tariffs placed on foreign nations that deplete America's "means of production" and keeps the middle class poor! The Federal Reserve was created to support American Economic policy; not destroy it! Either put people who will protect the American Worker with NEW GENERALS or abolish it!

America must have policies that protect and work for the workers and protect the family from poverty by an uncaring corrupt ruling elite!

Essay 8. Mortgage Bubble Breaks People: Government Fix Necessary!

Since 2006, the Mortgage Bubble deflated to such an EXTREME that America is still reeling from its effect. Greedy Wall Street Bankers in collusion with Government & Congressional Members used their positions to side step long accepted & proven practices to protect the American worker & homeowner from fraudulent schemes and practices. It is proven that those who will not learn from History, will repeat it and suffer the consequences of it! This Generation fits this scenario perfectly! SHAMEFUL!

The Law has been violated but where are the Prosecutions from law enforcement? Wall Street gets rewarded for their CRIMES!

So much needs be said about this American Tragedy that Obama, the Congress, Treasury & Federal Reserve by the FAILURES of former Chairman Alan Greenspan & Benard Bernakke has failed the AMERICAN WORKING FAMILY! During the Bush years, Treasury Secretary Hank Paulson, the Congress & President Bush allowed with the lack of oversight of the Federal Reserve the failure of watching monetary policy, checks and balances on mortgage lending resulting in the economic debacle since leaving office putting individuals and families at risk for their reckless and evil conduct!

THE IMMEDIATE NEED is to relieve the homeowner of foreclosure proceedings putting them at risk of losing their homes by paying the government for a direct intervention by the government into debt relief by removing the bad debt created by the mortgage bust putting homeowner's valuations below what they owe on their mortgages.

Then the homeowner would allow the government to pay off the existing mortgage to the Banks and Finance companys allowing it to take a 1st Deed of Trust so that the homeowner can pay the debt directly back to treasury and be **ABLE TO STAY IN THEIR HOME!**

THIS IS THE QUICKEST & MOST EFFICIENT WAY FOR THE ECONOMY TO REBOUND AFFIRMING FREE ENTERPRISE CAPITALISM DEFEATING & REPLACING CORPORATISM WITH ACCOUNTABLE & TRANSPARENT ACTS OF SOUND ECONOMIC POLICY THE FOUNDERS OF THE UNITED STATES INTENDED BE INACTED AS A STAPLE OF THE NATIONAL SECURITY INTEREST FOR THE AMERICAN WORKER AND THEIR FAMILIES!

Essay 9. **BALLONOMICS**: EMPOWERING THE MIDDLE CLASS FROM THE BOTTOM UP!

No discussion would be complete without weighing-in on the need to create economic prosperity with programs that assist people on all levels of their earning capacity. So far, we have discussed the need for Corporate Accountability on all levels of Society, that Business, Labor & Government at all levels be accountable to the people <> and move to create jobs by focusing the costs of production equal to that of other countries exporting their products into the

United States by inacting trade tariffs on those products
being exported/imported into America.

In other words, inacting a "dissinsentive" into the
"means of production" to disrupt the "ends of production"
of products being imported that have caused the trade
imbalance of manufacturing jobs out of the United States
relocated to other Countries at the expense of the
American Worker and their family that change comes!
3rd World Countries have learned from the mistakes of
others including the United States not to dilute their
economic base but empower it to give the opportunity
for family hegemony within their cultural base including
the parents of children who have the greatest demands
put on them in order to raise their children and save for
their retirement.

These countries have enacted monthly stipens to
the mothers to give their families an economic boost
to assist them with their children and family needs.
It says alot about how a country treats its children,
elderly & vulnerable. America is suffering economically
because of the attitudes it has assaulted its families,
children & parents and the people have allowed it to
happen! With the re-creation of MADE IN AMERICA
by lower Corporate Taxes and Trade Tariffs on Imports,
the Transfer of wealth between the American People
& OPEC Countries will Halt! With those savings and
continued growth and stability in the economy, the
Treasury will have a surplus to contribute monthly
to the well being of America's Families by & through

America's mothers because they know how to spend for their children and family's needs.

STIMULATE FAMILIES & YOU STIMULATE AMERICA!

Those eligible for Building Bridges To Prosperity must be assisted to train or retrain for jobs that will give our workers a hand up; not a hand out! This was one of the success stories started during the early 90's to assist people with job training to MAKE THEM PRODUCTIVE PEOPLE once again!

Now! with the reanactment of new policies that create $Billions$ of dollars in investment capital, the policies of the nation become more friendly and favorable to investing in our Society making our family's both ecnomically and personally strong once again! The family is the bedrock of the culture and it either rises or falls on how a nation treats it.

BALLONOMICS can be implemented any where in the world where there is sound monetary policy and a desire to serve the families who support their country. Lowering the Country's National Debt by giving the President the power to CUT SPENDING unilaterally on a line item vetoe, very important to impliment with Balanced Budget Amendment to the American Constitution increasing revenues by growing the economy to full employment & eliminating wasteful government spending with a stroke of a pen!

We have one of the most outrageous Corporate tax rates of the G20 Countries in the World. That must change so that we can re-establish an attitude of pro-business and pro-job creation for all legitimate business within all 50 United States to assist in the task of putting our people back to work! Cutting back the Corporate tax rate, eliminating the capital gains tax and allowing for total expensing of equipment and operational expenses makes it possible for any legitimate business to want to do business & invest in the American Job Market! Its time the Congress put Americans 1st once again!

Essay 10: STATE COURT PROBATE GUARDIAN ABUSE INJURES THE AMERICAN WORKING FAMILY!

As if there are not enough problems, worries and threats the American People has to encounter is that of State Court Probate Guardian Abuse! Because it has been a hidden tragedy for years by Judicial Officials & Officers who take an Oath to protect the vulnerable and infirmed; Society is finally beginning to understand the Criminal acts committed by those in positions of Authority who abuse, misuse and use their power to damage and destroy those they have taken an Oath to protect! As a result, many of the victims of Probate Abuse are a product of an uncaring, psychotic criminal enterprise plundering, pilferring and pillaging that person's life legacy into someone elses pocket without accountability nor consequence because of the acts by Corrupt Judges, Lawyers & Rogue Guardians. Most of these people are from the State Courts regardless of the State they reside.

The problem is so BIG that the US Attorney Office in every State of America could impanel a Grand Jury in each of the 50 States everyday. Our nation is emotionally & legally Bankrupt with Officials who are equally to blame for the demise of the American family. We call these parties, "easy buck artists" praying on the elderly & vulnerable waiting to die as Ward's of the State Court. Since the end of World War II, Americans that fought, died and created a great nation are now victims of their own Children! It is an American tragedy to say the least & demands an all out assault on Political Corruption at the highest levels of both State & Federal Government!

My own mother, Eleanor R. Ball fell victim to State Sponsored Guardian Abuse in Arizona during the time she resided at the end of her life. Both the State & Federal governments have known for years the corruption that is allowed in Arizona within its retirement community. They take your money, sell your property, isolate you from your family and drug you until your so incapacitated you die. Isolate, Medicate, Liquidate and then Terminate you. This Criminal Conduct goes unaccounted by a State Probate System in Pima & Maricopa Counties Arizona.

It has become a Public Safety Issue that Obama is

not willing to tackle nor any other law enforcement either. A National Tragedy has been created by the Children of the Great Depression/World War II Generation!

Now, I ask you my fellow Americans, "What place do you see yourselves in the future generations?" Are we to accept that which is unrighteous as thou it were righteous? Are we to teach our children that to get ahead in our family life is to Steal from our Neighbor regardless of the Consequences it may bring to them or to us? Are we to accept unrighteous acts as if they are righteous acts? Can we allow ourselves to cancel that which we know is wrong or accept it as if it were right?

THIS IS THE QUESTION THAT MUST BE ASKED OF THIS CURRENT GENERATION. IT CUTS RIGHT TO THE HEART OF THE KIND OF NATION WE HAVE BECOME & WHAT KIND OF NATION WILL WE BE?

Because of the State Courts, guardian abuse grows throughout the nation, the threat of it touching every working family in America. Current State Court Guardian proceedings in too many States have morphed into economic engines of Criminal Enterprise where the good guys are targeted by the System to be legally neutralized. The problem is a Real threat to your personal security and safety. It must be

ERADICATED! This is nothing less than what was fought against the Nazi's by our parents in World War II. To think that their own children may have adopted the policies of Nazi Pigs in Probate Proceedings is TOTALLY OUTRAGEOUS!

This cannot be allowed to continue without a very strong response by The People <>.

Thomas Jefferson said that State Tyranny grows when people grow tired and scared of their own government. The States have shown they cannot be trusted with the People's Business! Change is on its way! The American People will see to it or they will lose their Country and everything sacrificed, fought & died fore!

"Think 1st What Our Country Has Become, Act & Do What Must Be Done!"

Essay 11: Energy Policy Made New By Halting The Transfer Of Wealth!

Since 1973, the United States of America has been a hostage of the Oil Producing Nations of the World! In that year, many things happened to bring America to the brink of social, financial, political & economic ruin! Since then, the total some of all the events that have impacted the steady decline of America's People can be traced back to that year including the time the nation

went through the trauma of Vietnam & the
troubling 60's and political assassinations that
followed, an oil embargo and gas lines at the pump!

"WHY & HOW IS IT THAT AMERICA LIVES LIKE ITS 1973?"

Throughout our history, our nation continued to
create its own Crisis. Poor decisions, selfish motives,
bad behavior plague the United States of America.

FED UP? HAD ENOUGH?

The United States is broke because of a Corrupt
Political System of Self Interest that must go on a
STRICT SPENDING DIET! It also must halt the transfer
of wealth to Oil Producing Nations!

Free Enterprise Capitalism requires the flow of
money to support its needs and that of the family.
Stealing it is not earning it or having it come to you
by passive means. The American Dream is on tilt
because of years of unaccounted events that have
abused the American Family.

NOW, ITS TIME TO CHANGE IT & MAKE IT WORK FOR YOU!

AMERICA must finally get serious about moving to a
Green Economy. One where the "means of production"
are able to produce an equal supply and demand of the
products necessary to fuel a functional society. The
amount of Oil required to satisfy the enormous energy

needs of the United States can and will be satisfied by Solar Power. Electric motors that run on electricity, not fossil fuels have the best results to satisfy the needs & demands for American Energy & to halt the transfer of wealth from the American People to the Oil Producing Nations of the World, OPEC. America's debt could be eliminated by simply creating the cars, trucks and recreational vehicles to run on Solar Charging Systems both at the point of charging batteries and the skin on the car's roof to assist the motors and generators in the wheels.

In 1969, NASA put a man on the moon and a Lunar Rover completely dependent on batteries and solar power. Solar Power to homes too!

DON'T TELL ME IT CAN'T BE DONE!

America produces 7 million barrels of Oil a day. With the transfer to Solar Technology, America will have an Oil Surplus and be Energy Independent once again. America does not need to go broke on Oil imports. Neither does the American Family nor its children! Technology is here to free the American People & Halt the transfer of Wealth to Foreign Nations!

PART III-<u>REDEFINING AMERICA! THE NATION MUST PROTECT ITSELF!</u>

Essay 12: Foreign Policy And The Terrorist Threat:

<u>NO SHARIA LAW!</u>

Our Society was established, maintained and sustained by the blood of honorable men & women from the Halls of Montezuma to the Shores of Tripoli. They fought our nations battles on land & on the sea! Good People, let us NEVER FORGET THAT! Let us never forget the sacrifices that have been made by generations of Americans to keep our nation secure and economically free! The founders were concerned that monetary policy not be compromised by outside forces whomever and whatever they represented themselves to be.

Since 9/11, Overwhelming evidence shows that Muslim's in America are encouraged in replacing America's Constitutional Law with their own Sharia Law!

This is totally Unacceptable!

Mosques are being built at an alarming rate to complete this goal. It must stop and must be held as a risk against our Society! Our troops are in terriorist states while those who portray their interests parlay themselves in the United States.

Muslims have shown they are to be held suspect of their motives and Unamerican behavior regarding their communities.

The transfer of wealth to the OPEC nations has enabled those who are enemies of America to use our money to hurt our own people. It is another American tragedy that our People must take Seriously. Muslims have shown what they can do to society wherever they go. Europe is an Example of that. Sharia Law must go with those who support it opposite America's Constitutional Framework, fought, died and paid by the blood of our Valiant Men & Women!

"The President of the United States must never let foreign interests invade and take over this country but to protect its people and see that they are secure from evil in our own country!"

President Ball will not allow that to happen! Our heritage and our history should never be put at risk by the blood of so many who gave their lives for so many to be free from someone elses Tyranny!

The late Senator Barry Goldwater said in his nomination acceptance speech in 1964: "Extremism In The Defense Of Liberty Is No Vice!"- Cow Palace, San Francisco, California.

Soon afterward, Lyndon Johnson created a 60 second threat commercial enacting a "Daisy" Count down with a child holding a flower counting down the number of pedals with the detonation of an atomic device. This was used as a means to scare Americans to making them believe Goldwater would get them into a Nuclear War with the Russians. It was Richard Nixon who told his Chief of Staff Alexander Haig to get an atomic bomb ready to drop on Hanoi; not Goldwater!

"Politicians want people to believe that if you stand up to evil in all its forms, then something is wrong with you. Courage has only one name and its something you can't buy!" - Dennis Andrew Ball

Much can be said about the Islamic Jihadist Threat to America since 9/11. This is one of several important ones. As long as America's Southern border is porous to penetration by terrorists, America is vulnerable to threats outside its borders. Importing threats by order of the President is too.

Obama signed Presidential Order No. 2009-15 dated January 27, 2009 authorizing $20.3 million dollars for the migration of those Somalians to be flown to live in the United States with those who aspouse a similar Muslim dictum. What is so outrageous about this is that our own military is fighting the same attitudes in the middle east as those that are being allowed to multiply by this government in our own Country and with its support!

This my fellow Americans is a threat to the security of the nation and its law abiding citizens under our Constitutional form of American Government. No way will I allow a foreign entity to make safe haven in our Constitutional Republic Form of Government.

The Problems in Europe and Pakistan must not be allowed to happen here. The United States is a Free Zone regarding Islamic Extremists & Terrorists. We must be Vigilant to put down any threat that a foreign entity would tie our hands to hurt and injure our Men, Women & Children!

America is free to be who she is without the threat & fear by extremists pretending to be legitimate! Let them work for their children just as we work for ours! Let us take their guns out of their hands by demanding that business, labor & government in the middle east work for their families. Then you would see a change from within themselves toward their own families working for them diverting their hostile and negative teaching and attention away from the Societies of the World to make War causing their attention on themselves their children and families instead of KILLING innocent Civilians who have nothing to do with their ideology nor beliefs of total domination of the Free World!

Essay 13: Judicial Activism-Redefining Our Constitution Making Moot Our Bill Of Rights!

Common to most disputes are those within society responsible for their outcome and impact on the lives of the American People. It goes without saying, all the laws cannot change attitudes when those attitudes negatively impact on those who have taken an Oath to Protect those it was intended! This is the condition we find ourselves in today: JUDICIAL ACTIVISM.

Since 1789 only 8 Federal Judges have been removed from the Federal Judiciary. In many State Constitutions, NO Impeachment amendments exist to remove corrupt appointed or elected State Court, County Court or State Supreme Court Judges or Justices. Therefore, While the Rats are away, the Mice will play damaging the electorate and making our lives a Living Hell while the abuse of power continues by all manner of Judicial Misconduct heaped on the American Citizenry!

To make this STOP the American People must get busy and inact legislation in the State Legislatures of America making it an impeachable offense for Judges to break the law to be accountable as all Citizens of that State are accountable to both State & Federal Statues. It is a disgrace for an officer of the Court to be an outlaw of the law and still be able to practice and GET paid at the public's expense! No One Is Above The Law! But as the Law goes, so too goes those who use it to intentionally hurt those innocent & ignorant of it! In every division of State & Federal Court Proceedings, due process of law is abridged by Activist Judges who use their position in a corruptable fashion. This is a well known fact by the number of complaints filed by ordinary citizens to Boards of Judicial Review each year. If you don't believe it, then please look it up in every Jurisdiction of the United States of America.

A total disgrace of the Fifth & Fourteenth Amendments of the due process clause of the Constitution of the United States of America. Activists

Judges knowing the law is stacked against the citizens have betrayed the Constitution and use their office to hurt innocent and rob them of due process in Court filings!

"GET BUSY PEOPLE!"

Until these parties are held accountable by legislative process of the People, the abuse will continue! Get Busy People! The Bill Of Rights includes the Right of Due Process of Law. That Right is made moot by Judicial Misconduct that destroys our Rights and makes moot the outcome of many Decisions based on Equal Protection of Law upon the Citizens of our Great Nation! Our Bill of Rights becomes moot when Activist Judges are allowed to break the law and use the laws to hurt our people!

That is why it is essential the People get busy, enact legislation in the State Legislatures of America and enact the Election of all Judges TO THE BENCH and Removal of them by Impeachment provisions by Constitutional means including the removal of State Supreme Court Justices!

Federal Judges are held accountable by Impeachment! As a consequence, the greater tragedy is that those who practice law, they themselves become victims of the corruption either by participating in it or defending citizens of it.

They too become victims by being tagged by those practicing the corruption to be punsihed by the State Bar Association for fighting the corruption for their clients consequently being cited by the Courts and Punished by

It is a system completely out of control and ready to collapse on itself! America Has Grown In Trouble & So Have The American People, Before & After 9/11!

Essay 14: Reigning In The Sexual Revolution:
THE GAY AGENDA A REAL THREAT TO DESTROY TRADITIONAL AMERICAN FAMILIES BY MARRIAGE EQUALITY!

AMERICA is at a Crossroads that has been created by time and distance upon which its leaders have allowed others to travel. Prior to the Clinton Administration, the military of America had a policy that Gays/Lesbians would not openly serve in American Military Forces and if they were found out, they would be summarily dishonorably discharged! That began to change in the Clinton Administration with "Don't Ask, Don't Tell" that continued until the revocation by a Federal District Judge who ruled the policy was unconstitutional and must end.

That matter is still being considered by the Courts and may ultimately end up in the Supreme Court of the United States or Repealed by a Conservative President who believes in marriage & family integrity based on the definition of marriage as between a man and a woman; not same sex and not to be adopted within military ranks. It is totally gross to think two men legally married serving our Country in the military as openly Gay Partners and in the presence of heterosexual males who have totally opposite beliefs regarding family structure and function.

This is a recipe for total disaster within the integrity of military circles and the assault on the morale and spirit of the Armed Services! It is also a recipe for someone to get hurt within the ranks of active military personnel. The Gay/Lesbian Agenda knows no limits and because of that, Russia Arrests Gay/Lesbian Pride Leaders who Parade themselves openly as an acceptable lifestyle for their Society to adopt. The reality does not exist but is a choice made by both males and females to live same sex lifestyles contrary to the Nuclear Family and a conventional lifestyle between a man and a woman. This conflict between the sexes continues to fuel controversy within Western Society despite the rule of law and the wishes of the People. America is caught in a moral crisis created by its own people and allowed to grow by those in conflict with our heritage, freedom and example as a heterosexual, Judeo-Christian Nation.

The Gay/Lesbian Agenda wishes to alter that Structure to replace or include it as a legitimate alternative for American Society. This cannot be tolerated or allowed!

Gay Rights are not defined on the back of the American Constitution. The right to life, liberty and pursuit of happiness is abrogated by the Protections for Family Integrity by the Founders who never endorsed an alternative lifestyle as the norm for American Society. This is an abrogation of America's

it to continue to be the dominant model in Western
Society as America's norm for Society and the World!

The founders never intended to have Gays adopt
children from children of domestic violence to fill their
empty nests because of their same sex! The founders
never considered that American Democracy would be
predicated on same sex marriage brutalizing marriage
equality as synomous with one man one woman, the
true definition of "marriage".

The Scam has come from within the State Houses
of America; not its people!

In every case where the People have Voted,
Same Sex Marriage was voted down!

Every place where it has been adopted was not
by the people but by Gay Legislators with the
Support of Gay Judges who cramed it down Society's
Throat! This is an abuse of Judicial Authority and is a
Tyranny by the State!

The abuse is ongoing and must be eliminated by the
Nuclear Family! The people must get busy to introduce
leglislation and repeals Same Sex Marriage where it exists
and the affirming of the Defense of Marriage Act (DOMA)
so adopted in Federal Law.

Marriage is under attack by the Gay/Lesbian Agenda
between same sex partners. It threatens the Stability of
Society and the example of the Nuclear Family which is
Society's Norm.

In the Bible, Sodom & Gomorah were destroyed by

God for their Sin was great before the Moral Compass of God! America is a Great Nation because it has kept its moral compass consistent with that of God's Inalienable Rights coming from Him. God made Eve; not Steve! Remember, America is a Nation of People who has a moral conscience made in the image of God; not same sex! It is God who created the family and it is He who makes the rules; not men! Men are to follow God and obey His Commandments!   Also, God is not mocked!

Essay 15: THE TEN COMMANDMENTS:

God's Law For Society!

Shall America morph into a Godless Nation with no rules other than those created by man? It is a very timely question despite thousands of years of events and traditions that have shaped human kind.

Society is given a moral compass by God to follow and obey in their daily lives. It is what is necessary to keep a Great Nation morally, emotionally, personally, financially strong. We are told that in "God We Trust" may be inappropriate; that it is an Affront to the separation of Church & State.

God did design life to be taken and given freely to those who are responsible with it as His gift to his Creation. It behooves a Great People to observe and obey his ways. His Ten Commandments include the right to life and the punishment for taking it especially amongst the very innocent young and old alike.

God did not intend that man should suffer at the hand of other people, but to obey Him and honor the family which he created. It is written: "Honor Thy Mother and Father so that you may live a long and good life! In the absent of abuse, it is God's will that the family in America not only survive but thrive!

Certainly, as time and distance continue to make itself known in issues and events within American Society, the impact of bad behavior is having on the American Family is alarming! That is a hugh problem for sustaining our Republic & Democracy. The American Party of America/AOA & The ANC support our Godly heritage and traditions and believes that America is a blessed nation because God is put first and his laws that have governed Society for thousands of years.

The American Party & The People Support Them!

Essay 16: ILLEGAL Immigration:
The Demand For Enforcement & Reform!

AMERICA is a nation of Immigrants and has thrived by diversity of its Citizens who have contributed to her support and survival. Let us agree that a Great Nation requires a Great People! Many of those who have come here have gone thru the process of Legal Immigration. However, many have come here unlawfully, who violated our Immigration laws but may have contributed to our social needs. However, that is no excuse for them to break the law. Immunity is not an option to those who break the law and come to America illegally.

The position the party takes is that any immigrant who is brought illegally must be known and dealt with appropriately including deportation. It is not fair to the American Taxpayer to support illegal immigration at the cost of those who came here legally. Our laws are designed to be enforced.

It is the duty of the government to protect the American people from illegal immigration. Having opportunities for individuals to come to the United States to better themselves through work visa's is very needed and acceptable. Staying beyond their expiration date is not and purposefully having children in the United States while being here illegally or on a work visa is not.

The tax payers do not appreciate nor want to have to foot the bills of undocumented workers who use our system of social benefits to the detriment of our own people. Such practices make a mockery of our system of government and penalize hard working Americans with the burden of supporting those who won't. America was founded on a work ethic that has not changed since the founding of the Republic. It is important to remember that the American Worker is capable of producing as much if not more than any other working person in the World, if given the opportunity.

Jobs for working Americans must be protected

by Business, Labor & Government for the good of
the Community and Welfare of the Nuclear Family
Unit. It is our tradition and heritage as Made In
America Is Returned To The Forefront!

Essay 17: President Kenndy's Final Speech:
November 22, 1963! Dallas, Texas.

The Kennedy Speech as Written For The Trade
Mart in Dallas, TX. This is a special reproduction of
the Speech President Kennedy was prepared to
deliver but who's life was cut short by assassin's
bullets. Had President Kennedy survived and
allowed to proceed to fulfill his place in American
History, he would support this Party and its goals
because he was 1st an American and 2nd a Patriot!

"May his legacy live forever by his
Life, Service & Sacrifice!"

TEXT OF THE PRESIDENT'S SPEECH:

"I am honored to have this invitation to address
the annual meeting of the Dallas Citizen's Council,
joined by the members of the Dallas assembly --
and pleased to have this opportunity to salute
the Graduate Research Center of the Southwest.

It is fitting that these two symbols of Dallas
progress are united in the sponsorship of this

meeting. For they represent the best qualities, I am told, of leadership and learning in this city-- and leadership and learning are indespensible to each other. The advancement of learning depends on community leadership for financial political support and the products of that learning, in turn, are essential to the leadership's hopes for continued progress and prosperity. It is not a coincidence that those communities possessing the best in research and graduate facilities--from MIT to Cal Tech --tend to attract new and growing industries. I congratulate those of you here in Dallas who have recognized these basic facts through the creation of the unique and forward looking Graduate Research Center.

This link between leadership and learning is not only essential at the community level. It is even more indespensable in world affairs. Ignorance and misinformation can handicap the progress of a city or a company, but they can, if allowed in a foreign policy, handicap this country's security. In a world of complex and continuing problems, in a world of frustrations and irritations, America's leadership must be guided by the lights of learning and reason -- or else those who confuse rhetoric with reality and the plausible with the possible will gain the popular ascendancy with their seemingly swift and simple solutions to every world problem.

There will always be dissident voices heard in the

land, expressing opposition without alternative, finding
fault but never favor, perceiving gloom on every side
and seeking influence without responsiblity. Those
voices are inevitable. But today other voices heard in
the land -- voices preaching doctrines wholly unrelated
to reality, wholly unsuited to the sixties, doctrines that
which apparently assume that words will suffice without
weapons, that vituperation is as good as victory and
that peace is a sign of weakness.

At a time when the national debt is steadily being
reduced in terms of its burden on our economy, they
that debt as the single greatest threat to our security.
At a time when we are steadily reducing the number
of federal employees serving every thousand citizens,
they fear those supposed hordes of civil servants far
more than the actual hordes of opposing armies.
We cannot expect that everyone, to use the phrase
of a decade ago, will "talk sense to the American people."
But we can hope that fewer people will listen to
nonsense. And the notion that this nation is headed for
defeat through deficit, or that strength is but a matter
of slogans, is nothing but just plain nonsense.

I want to discuss with you today the status of our
security because this question clearly calls for the most
responsible qualities of leadership and the most
enlightened products of scholarship, for this Nation's
strength and security are not easily and cheaply
obtained, nor are they quickly and simply explained.
There are many kinds of strength and no kind will

suffice. Overwhelming nuclear strength cannot stop a guerrilla war. Formal pacts of alliance cannot stop internal subversion. Displays of material wealth cannot stop the disillusionment of diplomats subjected to discrimination.

Above all, words are not enough. The United States is a peaceful nation. And where our strength and determination are clear, our words need merely to convey conviction, not belligerance. If we are strong, our strength will speak for itself.

If we are weak, words will be of no help. I realize that this Nation often tends to identify turning-points in world affairs with the major addresses which preceeded them. But it was not the Monroe Doctrine that kept all Europe away from this hemisphere-- it was the strength of the British fleet and the width of the Atlantic Ocean.

It was not General Marshall's speech at Harvard which kept Communism out of Western Europe -- it was the strength and stability made possible by our military and economic assistance. In this administration also it has been necessary at times to issue specific warnings -- warnings we could not stand by and watch the Communists conquer Loas by force, or intervene in the Congo, or swallow West Berlin, or maintain offensive missles on Cuba.

But while our goals were at least temporarily obtained in these and other instances, our successful defense of freedom was not due to the words we used, but to the strength we stood ready to use on

behalf of the principles we stand ready to defend.

This strength is composed of many different

elements, ranging from the most massive deterrents

to the most subtle influences. And all types of strength

are needed -- no one kind could do the job alone.

Let us take a moment, therefore, to review this

Nation's progress in each major area of strength.

First, as Secretary McNamara made clear in his

address last Monday, the strategic nuclear power

of the United States has been so greatly

modernized and expanded in the last 1,000 days,

by the rapid production and deployment of the

most modern missle systems, that any and all

potential aggressors are clearly confronted

now with the impossibility of strategic victory --

and the certainty of total destruction -- if by

reckless attack they should ever force upon us

the necessity of a strategic reply.

In less than 3 years, we have increased by

50 percent the number of Polaris submarines

scheduled to be in force by the next fiscal year,

increased by more than 75 percent our

Minuteman purchase program, increased by

50 percent the portion of our strategic bombers

on 15 -minute alert forces.

Our security is further enhanced by the steps

we have taken regarding these weapons to

improve the speed and certainty of their

response, their readiness at all times to respond, their ability to survive an attack, and their ability to be carefully controlled and directed through secure command operations.

But the lessons of the last decade have taught us that freedom cannot be defended by stategic nuclear power alone. We have, therefore, in the last 3 years accelerated the development and deployment of tactical nuclear weapons, and increased by 60 percent the tactical nuclear forces deployed in Western Europe.

Nor can Europe or any other continent rely on nuclear forces alone, whether they are strategic or tactical. We have radically improved the readiness of our conventional forces -- increased by 45 percent of the number of combat ready Army divisions, increased by 100 percent the procurement of our ship construction, conversion, and our modernization program, increased by 100 percent our procurement of tactical aircraft, increased by 30 percent the number of tactical air squadrons, and increased the strength of the Marines.

As last month's "Operation Big Lift" -- which originated here in Texas showed so dearly, this Nation is prepared like never before to move substantial numbers of men in surprisingly little time to advanced positions any -- where in the world. We have increased by 175 % the

procurement of airlift aircraft, and we have
already achieved a 75 percent increase in our
existing strategic airlift capability.

Finally, moving beyond the traditional roles
of our military forces, we have achieved an
increase of nearly 600 percent in our special
forces -- those forces that are prepared to
work with our allies and friends against the
guerrillas, saboteurs, insurgents and assassins
who threaten freedom in a less direct but
equally dangerous manner.

But American military might should not and
need not stand alone against the ambitions of
international communism. Our security and
strength, in the last analysis, directly depend
on the security and strength of others, and that
is why our military and economic assistance plays
such a key role in enabling those who live on the
periphery of the Communist world to maintain
their independence of choice.

Our assistance to these nations can be painful,
risky, and costly, as is true in Southeast Asia today.
But we dare not weary of the task. For our
assistance makes possible the stationing of 3.5
million allied troops along the Communist frontier
at one-tenth the cost of maintaining a comparable
number of American soldiers. A successful
Communist break through in these areas,
necessitating a direct United States intervention,

would cost us several times as much as our entire foreign aid program, and might cost us heavily in American lives as well.

About 70 percent of our military assistance goes to nine key countries located on or near the borders of the Communist-bloc -- nine countries confronted directly or indirectly with the threat of Communist aggression -- Vietnam, Free China (taiwan) Korea, India, Pakistan, Thailand, Greece, Turkey and Iran. No one of these countries possesses on its own the resources to maintain the forces which our own Chiefs of Staff think needed in the common interest. Reducing our efforts to train, equip, and assist their armies can only encourage Communist penetration and require in time the increased overseas deployment of American combat forces.

And reducing the economic help needed to bolster these nations that undertake to help defend freedom can have the same disastrous result. In short, the $50 billion we spend each year on our own defense could well be ineffective without the $4 billion required for military and economic assisstance.

Our foreign aid program is not growing in size, it is, on the contrary, smaller now than in previous years. It has had its weaknesses, but we have undertaken to correct them. And the proper way of treating weaknesses is to replace them with strength, not to increase those weakensses by emasculating essential programs. Dollar for Dollar, in or out of government, there is no better form of investment in our national security than our much - abused foreign aid program. We cannot afford to lose it. We can afford to maintain it, we can surely afford, for example, to do as much for our 19 needy neighbors of Latin America as the Communist bloc is sending to the island of Cuba alone.

I have spoken of strength largely in terms of the deterrance and resistance of aggression and attack. But in today's world, freedom can be lost without a shot being fired, by ballots as well as bullets.

The success of our leadership is dependent upon the respect of our mission in the world as well as our missles -- on a clearer recognition of the virtues of freedom as well as the evils of tyranny. That is why our Information Agency has doubled the shortwave broadcasting powers of the Voice of America and increased the number of broadcasting hours by 30 percent, increased Spanish language broadcasting to Cuba and Latin America from 1 to 9 hrs. a day, increased seven-fold to more than 3.5 million copies of the number of American books being translated and published for Latin American readers, and taken a host of other steps to carry our messages of truth and freedom to all the far corners of the earth.

And that is also why we have regained the

initiative in the exploration of outer space, making an annual effort greater than the combined total of all space activities undertaken during the fifties, launching more than 130 vehicles into earth orbit, putting into actual operation valuable weather and communications satellites, and making it clear to all that the United States of America has no intention of finishing second in space.

This effort is expensive -- but it pays its own way, for freedom and for America. For there is no longer any fear in the free world that a Communist lead in space will become a permanent assertion of supremacy and the basis for military superiority. There is no longer any doubt about the strength and skill of American science, American industry, American education, and the American Free Enterprise System. In short, our national space effort represents a great gain in, and a great resource of, our national strength -- and both Texas and Texans are contributing greatly to this strength.

Finally, it should be clear by now that a nation can be no stronger abroad than she is at home. Only an America which practices what it preaches about (human) rights and social justice will be respected by those whose choice affects our future. Only an America which has fully educated its citizens is fully capable of tackling the complex problems and perceiving the hidden dangers of the

world in which we live. And only an America which

is growing and prospering economically can sustain

the worldwide defenses of freedom, while

demonstrating to all concerned the opportunities

of our system and society.

It is clear, therefore, we are strenghening our

security as well as our economy by our record

increases in national income and output --by

surging ahead of most of Western Europe in

the rate of business expansion and the margin

of corporate profits, by maintaining a more stable

level of prices than almost any of our overseas

competitors, and by cutting personal & corporate

income taxes by some $11 billion, as I have

proposed, to assure this Nation of the longest

and strongest expansion in our peacetime

economic history.

The Nation's total output- which 3 years

ago was at the $500 billion mark -- will soon

pass $600 billion, for a record rise of $100

billion in 3 years. For the first time in history

we have 70 million men and women at work.

For the first time in history average factory

earnings have exceeded $100 a week. For

the first time in history coporation profits

after taxes -- which have risen 43 percent

in less than 3 years--have an annual level

of $27.4 billion.

My friends and fellow citizens: I cite
these facts and figures to make it clear that
America today is stronger than ever before.
Our adversaries have not abandoned their
ambitions, our dangers have not diminished,
our vigilance cannot be relaxed. But now we
have the military, the scientific, and the
economic strength to do whatever must be
done for the preservation and promotion
of freedom.

The strength will never be used in pursuit
of aggressive ambitions -- it will always be
used in pursuit of peace. It will never be used
to promote provocations -- it will always be used
to promote the peaceful settlement of disputes.
We, in this country, in this generation, are --
by destiny rather than by choice -- the
watchmen on the walls of world freedom.

We ask, therefore, that we may be worthy
of our power and responsibility, that we may
exercise our strength with wisdom and restraint,
and that we may achieve in our time for all time
the ancient vision of "peace on earth, good will
toward men."

That must always be our goal, and the
righteousness of our cause must always
underlie our strength. For as was written long ago:
"except the Lord keep the city, the watchmen
waketh but in vein."

President John Fitzgerald Kennedy-

Dallas, Texas- November 22, 1963

Essay 18: Epilogue- Our Heritage & Our Future:

The Danger We Face!

Read what One hundred One Years before
the Death of President Kennedy was spoken by
one who knew the perils that could come to this
nation at the hands of unrighteous and evil men:

"I see in the near future a crisis approaching
that unnerves me and causes me to tremble for
the safety of my country....Corporations have been
enthroned and an era of corruption in high places
will follow and the money power of the country
will endeavor to prolong its reign by working upon
the prejudices of the people until all wealth is
aggregated in a few hands and the Republic is
destroyed." President Abraham Lincoln letter
to Colonel William F. Elkins, November 21, 1864.

"Now I am about a great journey where many
have traveled but few succeeded. If 100 Nations
wish to know me and 50 States Continue to Access
me, then those who are still waiting to find me are
only a cursor click away before the Entire World Will
Join Me That Which MUST Happen To Save The
REPUBLIC and make it Strong Once Again!" -
Dennis Andrew Ball, BALL2012.net, January 1, 2012.

My fellow Americans, we are engaged in a great battle for which the outcome is not certain for which the Crisis is Real! Can we do any less than generations past to secure the Common Good for those who sacrificed all to see that we are secure?

Let us journey together to make the World a Safer Place so that our children, and their children will have a Safer Place by which to raise our children and their children when we are long gone. We do this not because it is easy but because it is hard. Not because our lives have forgotten our past but because the past has caught the future in the cross hairs of history.

Let us pursue a course that brings us together that makes our voices one, and keeps our families secure for ourselves and those we love.

It is only fitting that we do this to honor those gone before us and that they are honored by our good deeds to those who need us most.

In the words of President Kennedy:
"Ask Not What Your Country Can Do For You,
Ask what you can Do For Your Country!".

I say: "Think 1st What Our Country Has Become,
Act & Do What Must Be Done!".

The Values that made America Great must return to the Land of Plenty to rediscover the treasure of Values that made Us Great! Sustainable Education that trains our people to do the jobs that make a difference in a Global Economy that attract talent throughout the World to do the jobs to not only invent but to sustain a leading edge within business, labor & government for the American People.

The Finest Minds that put people first and profits second valuing the American Worker and their family second to none. This is what I am talking about people!

Restoring and reinvigurating society to once again be accountable to God and each other. Protecting the Country from financial harm by electing leaders who put America 1st & Profits Second. Who demand a balanced budget amendment to the Constitution of the United States with term limits on their time of elected or appointed service.

Being kind to the environment and demanding reductions in the Carbon Emissions footprint by foreign countries and that of American Industry.

Prohibition on Fossil Fuel Production & Consumption with a massive restructuring promoting Solar Electrics, GeoThermal and Electric Vehicles that are perfected and used everyday to make America Energy Independent once again by taking out over 15,000,000 barrels of Oil a day of expensive foreign

Crude. It is past time for America to get real serious creating, maintaining and sustaining a Green Economy.

These are the kinds of initiatives & responses I see for Our Nation's economy both from within and without the United States of America! Its time that the People take back their Country and make it Safe & Secure for the Traditional Nuclear Family once again putting God back in the picture for without God in the picture, so says President Kennedy:

"the watchmen labor in vein!"

ABOUT THE AUTHOR...............

2012 Presidential Candidate, Dennis Andrew Ball is a "Natural Born Citizen" consistent with Article 2 Section 1 of the United States Constitution for eligibility to run for President of the United States. Born August 27, 1951 Los Angelos, California holds a Bachelors Of Arts Degree (BA) 1973, University of California San Diego, LaJolla, California. Major: Chinese History, Minor: Physics, Science, Technology.

Mr. Ball created the American Party Of America 1995 with the firm belief that Democracy that does not include the <u>best interests</u> of the traditional American Family cannot be sustained in a Plural Society. Therefore, the addage that Business, Labor & Government <u>must</u> work for the <u>best interests</u> of Children, Parents & Grandparents. This reality has the potential of also being exported to:

ALL THE NATIONS OF THE EARTH!

Thank you for your Vote & Support in 2012 to usher in
a new wave of thinking and behaving in our Corporate
& Political Culture in the United States of America!

Dennis Andrew Ball//s//BALL2016.net